SURRENDERING
to the VOICE
of GOD

JOAN LINNETTE DAVIS

ISBN: 978-1-7349439-8-6 Library of Congress Cataloging-in-Publication Date is available.
ISBN: 979-8-9876185-0-9

Project Specialist
Barlow Enterprises, LLC
Write Your Book Now! Visit: Text 478-227-5692

Legal Disclaimer
While none of the stories in this book are fabricated, some of the names and details may have been changed to protect the privacy of the individuals mentioned. Although the author and publisher have made every effort to ensure that the information in this book was correct at time of press, the author and publisher do not assume and hereby disclaim any liability to any party for any loss, damage, or disruption caused by errors or omissions, whether such errors or omissions result from negligence, accident, or any other cause.

Ordering Information
Surrendering to the Voice of God may be purchased in large quantities at a discount for educational, business, or sales promotional use. For more information or to request Rev. Joan Davis as the speaker at your next event, email: revjldavis21@gmail.com

Dedication

In loving memory of my parents, Uel Nathan Davis and

Josephine Rosemarie Davis, without whom I would not be who I am today. It is their beautiful humility, loving hearts, caring natures, immeasurable dedication, gentle patience, and God-fearing spirits that I have found to be admirable and an illuminating light in my life. I live my days to follow, with every step that I make a journey in purpose. Their foundation, example, and model of having a Christ-like mindset have taught me to trust God and be open to the calling God has for my life. A calling that I have witnessed them accepting in their lives, which has helped me to surrender to God's voice. It is because of their adorning light that I have learned to be unafraid to let my light shine, and now have the courage to do so as I continue to seek God's guidance and revelations along the way. I am forever grateful to them and the countless ways they have poured this knowledge into me. And for that, I thank and praise God for them, always.

Acknowledgments

I want to thank God, who is first in my life and the One who has inspired and equipped me spiritually to walk down this path to uplift, encourage, and strengthen others. It is God who equips me with everything right, to do the work He has called me to do that brings all glory to His Name.

To my professors at Palmer Theological Seminary, who have poured so much inspiration into my life throughout this Christian walk. You have supported me through your thoughtfulness, encouraging words, and one-on-one conversations, and empowered me to continue following God's guiding light rather than allowing my fears and doubts to consume me. Thank you for the prophetic words spoken over me that have reminded me that God has a purpose for me. Your teaching has taught me to believe in myself, to be full of confidence in the one who has sent me, and to always remember to "trust God and trust the process." Your words of encouragement have helped me hear God's voice and humbly submit to taking this journey of writing my first book. I am endowed with much gratitude and thankfulness for God allowing you to be a part of my life.

To my spiritual aunties, Sis Loraine Vance, Sis Linda Bradley, and Sis Loraine Council. Your prayers and words of delight have encouraged me to keep stepping forward on my journey to become a woman of purpose.

To my spiritual sister, Sis Mary Hall-Ulmer, for a bond ordained by God, which developed in our service of working alongside one another through the Youth and Young Adults Ministry at Mt. Zion AME Church in Norristown. The spirit of this unity has kept me strong and fervent.

To my spiritual brother, Bro Alton Jones (AJ), who has blessed me by always being available to give me big brother advice and help with my babies and grandbabies.

To my pastor, mentor, and father in the ministry, Reverend Carlos D. Bounds. My life has been rewarded by of your spiritual guidance, motivating push to keep pressing on, your encouragement not to allow anything to hinder me, encouraging conversations, testimonial expressions of wisdom, and prophetic words. I thank you for influencing me to accept my calling, what God was pressing upon me, and the overall direction in which He was moving me.

To my seminarian sister, December Pike, who reminds and encourages me that I can win, and told me to allow God's will for my life and His belief in me to override all my fears. It is time that I said yes. She also reminded me to allow the words found in Philippians 1:6 to be my anchor: "Being confident of this, that he who began a good work in you will carry it on to completion until the day of Christ Jesus." So I now shout, "Yes!" Thanks to my children, Noelani (Lani), Marlon, Myron, Nathan, and Milan, whose openness helps me to continue. My grandchildren Nathaniel (Nate), Paris, and Normani, whose smiles keep me going.

Contents

Encountering the Voice Of God

WHEN MY INNER BEING SPEAKS

When I reflect on our encounter, I was surprised by the way You moved what You had created to get my attention. My devotion I gave to You always, but that day was different from other days. I got up from my knees after our time spent together in beautiful devotion that morning. The essence of that day was illuminating, but I could not tell why until I stepped outside my door onto my porch. It was in that instant, while standing there, that I glanced up to the heavens toward You and you allowed me to see the movement of Your power casting out before me and resting upon my face. A resting upon my face that left me astonished by Your glory and the radiance of who You are. You consumed me. I was mesmerizing as you reminded me that I was not by myself.

You, directed my eyes to look up toward You so that You could display Your power upon me. Consumed by Your splendor, I saw a patch of dark clouds that was compelling. Nonetheless, no sooner had I seen those dark patches of clouds, You performed a marvelous miracle before my eyes. In Your loving, sweet voice, You uttered to me, "My daughter, my child, I just wiped away all those dark days." Immediately, those dark clouds moved away and tears streamed down from my face.

As the tears continued to flow from my eyes, I felt Your warm presence surrounding me. I knew then that I would never feel alone again. The things that once were burdensome in my life had been lifted. I thought I was forgotten, but You revealed that You were always listening. You knew the prayers I prayed and the tears I cried. You understood how deeply my spirit had been broken. All the while, when my questions of why it was happening to me were not answered, I felt alone and abandoned. But that day, You entered into my sadness and made me whole again—a true sign that You had and would always be concerned about me.

From that sweet encounter with You, I was able to experience the power of transformation and restoration. You exposed my inner brokenness and allowed me to see that it would hinder me no longer, for there was much you had to reveal and do through me. My inner being had been restored and the rivers of Your love flowed through me. I was made anew that day, and my concerns were no longer all-consuming. I was no longer concerned about the hurt and pain. I was no longer worried about the stains of yesterday. I was no longer troubled by the lack of money in my account bank, which had run dry. I had your assurance that everything was going to be better than before. That morning's unforgettable devotion assured me of that. Even though what I'd experienced in my life was real, and at times difficult to bear, I was reminded that I could put my full trust in You.

In You, I can trust always, for your words reminds me: "Fear not, for I am with you."

Introduction

FEAR NOT, MY CHILD

"Fear thou not, for I am with thee; be not dismayed;
for I am thy God: I will strengthen thee; yea, I will
help thee; yea, I will uphold thee with the right hand
of my righteousness."
– Isaiah 41:10 (KJV)

Life experiences can make you feel too inadequate to accept the call God is sending to you. This is especially true when you look at all that has happened in your life, and when the weight of life has consumed and caused you to feel discouraged. So, you say to yourself, "How can God be calling *me*, knowing where I have come from, where I have been, and what I have done? What would the Lord possibly want with *me*?" But I can remember the Lord saying to me, "Fear not, my child, for all things are working together for your good. I will be with you always. I will carry you into those places that have been predestined a long time ago, and no weight of life will hinder my plans for your life. So again I say, fear not, my child."

I was truly amazed at what the Lord had spoken, which took my breath away. But even with God's reassurance, I could not help but to question at times. "Why me, God? How can I, God? Why is it so difficult for me to surrender to Your voice, God? Why am I allowing my life experiences, the weight of it all, to consume so much of my life? Why am I allowing it to make me feel that I am not qualified to be called by God? Why am I feeling so unworthy to be amongst the elected and proclaim the Good News of Jesus Christ?" I know that I am not the only one who has asked these questions and felt this way. I feel so afraid, but God will not stop speaking to me. I am constantly wrestling with God's call for me to surrender to His voice. I am constantly wrestling with feelings of inadequacy. And this is why!

From my beginning until now, God has been working His purpose in my life. I can see that now, when I look back over my yesterdays. I was born in the parish of St. Ann's Bay on the Island of Jamaica, West Indies, to Uel and Josephine Davis. I am the oldest of my siblings. My parents were both faithful believers. My father was the preacher in our church, and loved serving and telling others about Jesus Christ. He was not afraid to share the Gospel with others, regardless of their denomination. He was gifted with the knowledge of the Scriptures in the Bible. His experiences went beyond just understanding the Scriptures. He could quote Scripture verses without opening the Bible, and before you located that verse of the Scripture. My mother was an evangelist in our church. She was gifted, especially in the gift of speaking of tongues and discernment. She had a prophetic gift and was able to tell others what God was saying or doing for them. Their strong commitment to Christ Jesus stood out to me as a child traveling side by side with them as early as the age of two.

Growing up I learned many things from my parents in regarding to their beliefs in Jesus Christ, all of which set the foundation of my faith and helped me grow richer in it. I learned three valuable lessons that I felt they demonstrated in their lifetime: their relationship with God, their relationship with family, and their relationship with the community. Their values influenced my life and how I developed my relationship with God. Why? Because it all started at home with my parents through prayer, Bible study, and a daily commitment to studying the Word of God for our personal growth. We prayed as a family every morning and evening, and we had daily devotions. We worshipped on Saturday, which was known as the Sabbath. It started from sunset on Friday and lasted until sunset on Saturday and served as a time committed to total devotion and worship of God. The keeping of the Sabbath was a very strict practice in my home. There was no cooking, no use of the microwave, and no watching television until sunset on Saturday evening. During this time, our family was committed and dedicated to God's prayer, studying the Bible, and worshipping God through hymnals and other musical selections. We were all participants in those prayers, practices of studying the Word of God, and worship expressions through songs. These moments instilled in me a reverence to honor, worship, and to continually seek to have a personal relationship with God. The adoration for God that my parents placed inside of me became monumental in my life as a Christian believer. As a woman of God, those disciplines, anchored and showed me how to live a life of faith.

Having a firm foundation in Christ was necessary for our life, as my parents showed it, along with the significance of having a relationship with our family. My parents always believed in the importance of helping others, whether they were a family member or a stranger, because Christ believed in serving others, as displayed in His earthly ministry. It was believed that we should have this Christ-like attitude toward others to adopt Jesus Christ's model. This explains why I am so deeply rooted in my family and opening myself to others. I have spiritually adopted so many people to be a part of my family and shared my love and pearls of wisdom with them. I have come to understand the joyful smiles that were imprinted on my parents' faces and are now mirrored in my life.

The values my parents taught me have governed my life, from seeing the importance of knowing God to extending a love of service to others, which goes beyond my family to others. Even more important is the need to go out into the world and minister in places of brokenness, even at the cost of rejection. I saw my parents do this work—a work of splendor and honor to God in their eyes. In my eyes, those notable acts that were worth being celebrated were not always appreciated and respected by others. I recall many struggles in my parents' lives when it came to serving people in our community. Struggles that I could never quite understand, but that left my parents hurting. Still, they kept enduring through it all, and even helped people who never really appreciated them, although I never could understand why. How could they continue to help the same people who hurt and mistreated them over and over again? I can recall asking my dad, "Why do you continue to help others when you are being treated unkindly?" He said to me, "Joan, I do it because we are here to help one another without looking for anything in return. Because God teaches us to be kind and helpful to one another." I did not understand what that meant at the time, but I know now that he hoped I would understand it one day. It was not clear at the time because my eyes saw something else.

I saw the constant struggles, the offenses, and the ill-treatment they experienced. Seeing them endure those adversities bothered me to my core. I felt defenseless in resolving it, but my parents saw something greater. I continued to watch my dad, armored with strength, continue his efforts to be a fervent servant of the Lord. The same was the case for my mom. She moved forward with a good attitude and a spirit of resilience and humility. Furthermore, she never stopped serving. She would prepare meals for any visitors who came by our home. Using the best dinnerware we had, my mother set the table as though it were a holiday celebration. She never murmured any complaints or dismay, but served as she believed would be glorified in the Lord's sight. She never looked for anything in return because she knew her virtue would be rewarded by God. They both aimed to be the light spoken about in the Bible, and for that light to be evident when they were seen taking care of God's people. They looked for nothing in return. That, they believed, the world could not give to them. However, they knew that God alone would reward them on the other side of glory. I had true admiration for their character, conduct, behavior, and lifestyle, as well as for the light that burned deep within them. Truly, their light was shining for all to see, and was not hidden. My parents had attributes I hoped to possess as I journeyed in my daily Christian walk. And that undeniable light that shone bright in their lives never dimmed, even when going through the heaviness of lows. I wanted that same light to illuminate my life and teach me how to disallow the difficulties of life to dim my light in any way, but to keep it shining bright for all to see, just as God intended it to be.

The light of Christ was present in the life of my parents and served as a guide to teach me how to live my life, regardless of what may be happening. Now it is my responsibility and an act of faith to build my dependence on Christ, who enables me to press through it all like my parents showed me to do in their walk as faithful believers. My trust must be in Christ alone because nothing can be done or achieved apart from Him. When I think back to experience that happened in July of 1987, this message is so clear. I was fifteen years old when my family relocated to the United States. We were in a different country and the United States was different from our culture but the shift and change in location neither changed our belief system, nor did our feet waver from that foundation that was built in our understanding of who Jesus Christ was. We remained constant in our belief and conduct. Our cultural belief and commitment to the doctrine of God did not change within my family. My parents' expectations and their standards were still high. They enrolled me in a Catholic high school and my dad made very clear his views when participating in different services of the school. He said that I would attend the classes but would not participate in most of them. This showed how strong, firm, and compelled he was to uphold the standards and belief systems he believed were true and that he was serious about making sure that we did the same. I had to adhere to the rules no matter what.

These values still direct my life, even today. Serving and reverencing Christ is to be placed first and above all else.

I was new at the high school, and new in this country, and I lost my dad in my junior year. I was devastated. I felt like everything in life had been taken away from me. I was at a low point in my life. I was trying to figure out how to get through the devastation of it all. While resting in the dark silence of sadness, I remembered the words of my parents: "Talk to God about it." I was reminded to talk with God through prayer about what I was feeling and experiencing at the time. This is not always easy to do when you are overwhelmed by the gloominess of hurt, but I rested at God's feet. In meditation, God spoke to me and gave me what I needed to find the strength to return to things, one day at a time. I wasn't ignoring what I felt or denying the emptiness that was there, but God reassured me that everything would be okay. I was able to return and finish high school within a certain time frame. I still was gloomy, but God kept saying, "Just remember what I said." And from there, I had the strength to endure and push through. I thank God for giving me the strength to press through the grief. Besides, people were looking to me for strength because I am the oldest of my siblings. My strength was what my family rested upon, and I did what was necessary to be strong for them. I did everything from helping my mom in the house to helping my siblings with their work to being that shoulder to rest on when it was needed. I always had an ear that was open and ready to listen. But most of all, I had to be the voice that reminded everyone to keep our eyes on God.

My family did not escape having the deal with the sorrow we all felt from losing my dad, but I saw God's favor and presence around us as the years passed on. We learned to lean so much on each other, and drew closer to one another so that we'd never forget the memories we had of my dad. Eventually, the days be brighten up for us, only to become dark once again when my mother became ill and was diagnosed with kidney failure. She was placed on dialysis and received treatments three times per week. During her illness, the family was in danger of losing the family home. I was grateful to God at a young age for the confidence to advocate for my mother and siblings while taking the position as family caretaker. Many obstacles came about along the way but the obstacles caused me to continue to seek after God, because it was not easy to bear alone. In my seeking after God, He made His presence known to me. I could feel the presence of God moving all around me and working on our behalf. Though the problems we faced were strong, God showed Himself to be stronger. We did not have to leave our home. God continued to provide for us and satisfy our needs. His grace was truly sufficient in our lives.

God is loving. We experienced His touch as He carried us through. His touch never left us, but held us up in our times of trouble and even after losing my mother a few years after my father had transitioned. Both parents were now gone. Again, our family felt the weight of grief resting on our house. I was a single mother raising a two-year-old daughter at the time, and now had the responsibility of caring for my younger siblings, who were ten and thirteen years old. I felt all was gone away from me. Honestly, I did not know what was next. All I could see was fear, doubt, and worry creeping up into our home. To make matters worse, I was feeling that same sense of overwhelm on the inside. It would not leave my mind. The physical presence of our parents was gone. The ones who were our light and strength were not there to lean on. Now, we only had each other. I had to be strong for my daughter and my siblings. I knew that I could not give up. I found myself having to move forward without knowing what the next step would be. Seeking God's guidance during those most difficult times was all that I could do.

Using the foundation of my parents' faith, I developed a personal relationship with God. I asked Him to cover me the same way He covered my parents. I reflected on what my parents had taught us growing up. Keep your mind focused on God, stay in constant prayer, worship, and praise your way through life's storms, find comfort and strength in studying the Word of God, and never stop trusting in the Lord no matter what your circumstances are. Trust in God always, for He is the rock and foundation of your life. This is what I kept thinking about and innocently hearing the voice of my parents telling me to do. I embraced the Holy Spirit for strength as He guided me in raising my daughter and my siblings. I was comforted, and my strength renewed. But still, at times, I doubted and felt lost because it was a lot to handle on my own.

As a single mother raising my daughter and my siblings, it seemed at times, that the weight of life was beating up on me even the more. As a family, we attended church and kept at least the foundational belief of my parents. However, with all that was happening, my relationship with God was not at the place at which I could truly and clearly hear His voice. I knew the importance of having a relationship with God and sharing that truth with others. But I cannot deny the fact that it was a struggle. As time continued, I met someone who, after two years of dating, asked me to marry him. In our marriage, we discussed our beliefs. I shared my beliefs about the Christian lifestyle I was raised to believe in and told him I wanted those same values reflected in our home with our family. We started attending church together like my parents had done, as a family. Through this union, God blessed us with twins—a boy and a girl. Soon after, however, we separated. And again, unhappiness was at my door.

This was yet another obstacle in my life and another moment of uncertainty. All that I had once believed and dreamed about marriage was fading away. The picture of marriage I dreamed of was erased. It was not the wedding that I dreamed of for my family. Nor was it the story from the pictures I had created and imagined in my mind. The experience made me feel empty and my heart was shattered once again. I decided that there was no other place to go but to God. I sought after Him to fill my emptiness, and to fulfill my needs—no place or person could provide for me like God. So, during my separation, I rested heavily again at God's feet and learned that I needed Him to be first and foremost in my life. I needed to be on the path that God had for me. Everything else seemed to be nothing more but than a sad song. But in Him, I found myself and everything else that I truly needed.

I had turned in so many directions, but all my feet could do was stumble and cause me to fall. My reflection in the mirror let me know that I needed something more for my life than I could find on my own. In 2013, I found myself at an evening worship service, sitting with a heart of uncertainty and an empty inner cup, looking for something to fill me up. I needed something to make my days brighter and a bit more hopeful. I was searching for something more. My mind was consumed with so much, but secretly longing desperately for something supernatural to happen to me that would turn my sadness to happier days. I heard an invitation being made by the pastor of the church. I can still hear her voice like it was yesterday. She said, "If you know God is calling you to ministry, come up, and He will do the rest."

Looking back, I am not sure how I reached the altar. Now that I understand the plan of God, it is clear that I was ready to surrender it all. It was time for me to yield to the voice of God. The Holy Spirit was prompting me to finally surrender to Him at the altar, and to stop holding back. As I stood at the altar, I looked into the pastor's eyes and said, "I want to be an Evangelist."

Just thinking about this moment, I am taken back to when God says to the Prophet Jeremiah, *"Before I formed thee in the belly I knew thee; and before thou camest forth out of the womb I sanctified thee, and I ordained thee a prophet unto the nations."* [Jeremiah 1:5 (KJV)] I knew at that moment that I was always in God's plans. He had a plan for my life, and it had been revealed to me. It took some time for me to realize what the plan was, but it was made clear to me that day. Ever since, I have been moving forward in the vision God planned for me. I thought, when I answered my calling to the ministry to become an Evangelist, that this was all God had for me. However, I quickly learned that being an Evangelist was not all that I would do. God's plan for me involved so much more.

In June of 2015, I felt God was calling me to a higher charge in the ministry. I sat with the pastor of the church and shared with her what I felt God was calling me to do. She shared with me that the Holy Spirit was showing her something uplifting and empowering concerning the ministry and me. After a long conversation and confirmation, I applied to Palmer Theological Seminary in July 2015. I was accepted into the Master of Divinity program and started in August 2015. I was on my journey to achieving my Master of Divinity, which was the result of my response to answering the call to go into pastoral leadership. As I began to operate in my calling, and saw the value in this journey. It was affirmed again and again that there was something God needed *me* to be in this world. So, I walked in that direction, only to learn that no journey (even the right journey) exempts you from trials and tribulations.

I have come to the realization that no journey is ever an easy one. On the contrary, obeying the voice of God also requires you to fight and to keep believing that the journey you said yes to was meant for you. No sooner had I started my studies, I was faced again, like many others in life, with challenges. I lost my car. My children and I were on the verge of being homeless. I sought more of God's guidance once again. Surely, God did not fail me. In fact, I experienced the faithfulness of God. I had many deep conversations with God, reminding Him of His promises and my obedience to His calling.

One morning, after my devotional time with God, I walked out of the door onto my porch and sat, waiting for my ride to class. A dark patch of cloud was lying over my porch. I turned my eyes towards the sky. The dark clouds began to separate and it was then when I heard the voice of God say, "I just wiped away your dark days." Right then and there, I knew God was up to something greater. My response to Him was, "Thank you, Jesus." From that day forward, I never forgot that God would be with me always. In God's perfect timing, I was blessed with a car. A few days later, my children and I were moving into another house. The rent was less and the space was comfortable for my family. God reminded me in all of this that He cared for me and that His love was real. He reminded me that I should never forget His word:

"Fear thou not, for I am with thee; be not dismayed; for I am thy God: I will strengthen thee; yea, I will help thee; yea, I will uphold thee with the right hand of my righteousness."

- Isaiah 41:10 (KJV)

Looking back on all that I have had to experience in my life, I genuinely believe our challenges and obstacles do not take away the fact that God promises to take care of us. Although my challenges were overwhelming, God always showed up and kept His promises to me. And He continuously does what He promised in my life. So, to all who will read this book, I pray it will help you understand and allow God to direct and speak to you.

Now let us take the journey.

Chapter One

HEARING THE VOICE OF GOD

He that hath ears to hear, let him hear.
- Matthew 11:15

It can be difficult to hear God's voice when life's storms are beating against you and you are overtaken by the many troubles in your life. Circumstances can consume your mind, time, and energy and make it impossible at times to focus on anything let alone on hearing the voice of God despite all of the things that clutter your mind. This can be a challenge for anyone. I know, because I have been there before. I know how much of a struggle it was to be connected to anything other than my problems. I have found that in those tough times and overwhelming moments of uncertainty, you find yourself questioning, "Am I in the place to hear His voice? And how can I?" When you just cannot seem to rest from the countless situations you are faced with, the constant worrying, the unshakable feels of anxiety, the swelling heartache, and throbbing headaches because of constantly rewinding day after day the things in your mind that will not allow you to ignore what you are going through. So how is it possible to hear anything? It is all right to feel that way and it is all right to question these things. You will not be the last to wrestle with these same concerns and thoughts. The blessing is that God is still able to push His way through all of the mess and filter it all out so you can have a personal encounter and connection with Him. Sometimes it just requires that you learn how to be still. To be still does not mean that you ignore what is happening in your life, but that you make the time to say, "Lord, here I am!"

Life's battles can be heavy and exhaust us all. So it is understandable that we feel the way we feel in those moments. All that I was enduring and working through in my life did not make it easy for me to hear God trying to speak to me. I was there! I have been in those places and moments when the weight of life's difficulties consumed me so much that it left no room for me to seek God for His guidance. Nevertheless, the Word of God says, *"But seek ye first the Kingdom of God, and His righteousness, and all these things shall be added unto you."* Matthew 6:33 (KJV)

By deciding to figure things out on my own rather than making the time to hear God's voice to help me through those dark and gloomy trials that never seemed to let go of me, I'd placed myself in a problematic position. But what I came to learn, and what you will come to recognize for yourself, is that in order to be in a position to hear God's voice, you have to spend time praying, studying His

Word daily, meditating in silence at His feet, and being present. This will help you get into the presence of God. He wants to be in partnership with each of us. He does not want us to have to bear things alone. This is why it is important to take the time to pray and study the Word of God: to keep us connected to Him. I the Bible Jesus reminds us, *"I am the vine, ye are the branches: He that abideth in me, and I in him, the same bringeth forth much fruit: for without me ye can do nothing."* John 15:5 (KJV)

So ask yourself: "What will it take to be in position to hear God's voice?" The Lord would have me tell you to come into partnership with Him and make Him your primary source. Once you have a connection with Him, you open yourself to having a new life in Him, because of your willingness to open yourself, to be poured into by God and begin a new path of spiritual growth. You will no longer look at your problems and situations the same way. Now that you have realized that God is on your side and has always had a concern about you, you are in line to hear His voice and allow it to guide you through those challenges of life that once weighed you down. Take it from me; I had to come to this point in my life because I was tired of feeling exhausted and being weighed down by the problems that were so overwhelming for me.

I learned to stop placing limits on God and started seeking His guidance. By allowing God to be in control, I was able to see the possibilities of change in those challenging circumstances. I learned the value of scheduling quiet time to be in the presence of God, and of blocking out everything that was trying to take control of me, because I was desperate for anything other than hardship and feelings of brokenness. Eventually, it became much easier to hear God's voice. I can recall, in one of my quiet times with God, where He directed me to read the Book of Job. At first, I had no clue: Why the Book of Job? However, I followed God's direction and started studying Job, only to come to learn that I was not the only one with troubles that come rushing into a life time and time again, one after the other. In the story of Job, I found my strength, which helped me deal with my challenges *and* keep praising God, despite the pain from those situations. I was assured of His protection.

To this day, I still find myself going back to the Book of Job as a reminder that God is in control. I encourage you to seek God and find some quiet time to spend with Him in prayer. Continue praying and studying His word. I guarantee you that no matter what challenges you are facing, He is in control and will carry you through it all. Never forget that He is with you and He will guide you, as long as you keep yourself in the place and in the position to hear His voice.

Meditation

The prompting of God's voice has a purpose. God is reaching out because He has a purpose for you, but is seeking to help your work through some things in your life so you can reach the fullness of what has been predestined. He is trying to take you to where He wants to send you to be a blessing, a means of inspiration, a voice of encouragement, and a vessel of strength to help others through their problems. What God needs is for you to allow Him to remove your doubts and fears. You must surrender everything to Him. These distractions must be removed so that he can position you to hear His voice more clearly.

God speaks in so many different ways because He shares a language with those He created. He has many ways of speaking directly to us which become more clear as we draw closer to and develop our relationship with Him. The language is beautiful and we are able to identify God's voice separate from all else. He wants us to recognize His voice so that He can use us to speak for Him. For some of us, God speaks through songs, to others by reading a book, and to some He speaks when they are being still in the moment. Whatever way

God uses to get our attention, once we hear from Him, He can use us to speak for Him. The Bible tells us how God used the prophets to be His voice to speak to the people. For example, He used Jeremiah to warn the people so they could turn from their wrong ways. Similarly, Jonah was used to warn the people of Nineveh of its coming destruction and Moses was used to free the Israelites from the bondage of slavery with Pharaoh. Whatever means God uses, we must be ready to hear where He is telling us to go. We have to be free from that which distracts us and makes us feel inadequate to serve. We must be completely turned toward God in order to hear and receive.

I pray that you will be in a position to hear from God the plans He has for you.

Reflection

How has it been challenging for you to surrender to God's voice in your life?

_____

_____

_____

_____

_____

Have you been exhausted by the problems in your life that have made it seem as though God is so far away?

_____

_____

_____

_____

Discovering God

Sometimes, life experiences can make it difficult to surrender to God, because we feel that our brokenness will be exposed and our shame revealed, and we fear that we will be judged by others. But what I have come to learn as that when you surrender to God's voice, you will overcome your challenges with His help. His promises assure us of that "Yes, I am with you. Yes, I will carry you. Yes, I will hold your hand." Now, I encourage you to seek God as you surrender to His voice in your life.

Scripture

Psalm 37:5—"Commit the way unto the Lord; trust also in Him; and He shall bring it to pass." (KJV)

2 Corinthians 12:10—"Therefore I take pleasure in infirmities, in reproaches, in necessities, in persecutions, in distresses for Christ's sake: for when I am weak, then am I strong." (KJV)

Isaiah 41:13—"For I the Lord they God will hold thy right hand, saying unto thee, Fear not; I will help thee." (KJV)

Prayer

Heavenly Father, I come to You, thanking You for the things You have and continue to do for me. Lord Jesus, I ask You to teach me what it means to surrender to Your voice. Being obedient to Your voice, answering Your ways, committing to Your will, is all I desire. Father, I seek You more. Help me to know more about what it means to trust in You. Help me do what You ask of me, rather than fearing the unknown. Help me learn what it means to be open to Your will so that you can be glorified through me, Father. Let the words of my mouth and the meditations of my heart be acceptable in Your sight. I pray this prayer believing it is done, in Jesus' name. Amen, amen, and amen.

Chapter Two

RESISTING THE VOICE OF GOD

Behold, I stand at the door, and knock: if any man hear
my voice, and open the door, I will come in to him, and
will sup with him, and he with me.

– Revelation 3:20

As God was leading me through this discussion about the

struggles that we have in hearing His voice, I was reminded that often, we can hear the Lord speaking to us, but for whatever reason, we turn away from His voice. People turn away because things are distracting them. They fear doing what God is calling them to do. They do not feel adequate to live out their calling. They are too consumed by the cares of the world and what people might think of them. The list can go on and on. So, God said to me, go to the dictionary and look up the word *resistance*.

The Merriam-Webster dictionary defines *resistance* as "of, relating to, or being exercise involving pushing or pulling against a source of resistance (such as weight) to increase strength."

God is calling out to us and knocking at our door, but we turn away as though we do not hear Him calling, can't believe He is calling us, or have allowed something to get in the way that keeps us from hearing His voice. I know this to be true, because I experienced moments of resistance in my life when I knew God was calling me. I fought countless times with God, but I realized in those battles that resisting His voice can place us in an uncomfortable position. This awkward and uncomfortable position can add to our doubts and fears. And it cannot be denied that I had a number doubts and fears when I was struggling to surrender to God's voice. I remember reading in the Bible, where the Apostle Paul in the Book of Timothy says, "For God hath not given us the Spirit of fear, but of power, and of love, and of a sound mind." 2 Timothy 1:7 (KJV) So, regardless of what we might feel and why we might feel that way, God still expects us to take heed to what He says. He is trying to get our attention by calling out to us. Wherever we are or whatever we might be doing or even going through, God is calling our name. Our weapon against the doubts and fears that the enemy is always handing us is to spend time with God daily. Study His Word, talk to Him about the things we are struggling with, and make prayer a lifestyle practice. Learning to be still in the presence of God will help us overcome the doubts and fears that the enemy brings to our thoughts so that we can focus our attention completely on God.

My life's struggles became extremely challenging when I knew God was calling me into the ministry. I did not find it to be an easy thing to accept. I had my reasons for why I turned my back on God and ignored His call. Though God, in His longing for me, did so many things to get my attention, I just refused to listen. I was not like the Prophet Samuel, who, in his response to God calling him, said, "Here I am." That was not me. My friends, as well as my pastor, kept saying to me, "God has not given us the spirit of fear." Spiritually, I was not in a place to hear whatever they were saying, nor did I want to receive what they said. My thoughts at the time were that I was trying to do what God had asked of me at one time, but because I was faced with so many challenges, I refused to go any further in my spiritual walk at the time. I was tired of being burdened by so much. I believed that God should be with me, but I was blinded by the experiences that were drowning me.

I was wrong. It was not that God did not hear my cries, but doubt and fear overshadowed my faith and caused me to believe that God was not understanding. This caused me to become resistant to listening to the voice of God. I just felt so far away and deep in my depression that it was so hard to see the light. I wept so much and wondered when the joy of seeing the morning was going to come. Everything seemed dark, as if there was no way out for me. I had gone so deep, but I was in time reminded that the depth of it all could not keep me away from God's love.

So I began talking with God, because I wanted to understand the struggles that I was facing. But above all, I wanted to be freed from it all. I stopped resisting and started listening to His voice. And while being in the stillness of His presence, God led me to fast for seven days. I was led to pray and drink pure, clear water. He took me through 180 degrees of cleansing—a new level of learning to listen to His voice. I learned in the stillness of God's presence to stop listening to the inner doubts and fears that were preventing me from listening to His voice. I learned the beauty of prayer and obedience to the voice of God. My fears and doubts lessened the more I stopped letting the enemy deter me from pushing toward the plans God had for me. Finally, I listened!

Your Prayer Life

The Scriptures say, *"And ye shall seek me, and find me, when ye shall search for me with all your heart."* Jeremiah 29:13 (KJV] It also says, *"Rejoice evermore. Pray without ceasing. In everything give thanks. For this is the will of God in Christ Jesus concerning you. Quench not the Spirit."* 1 Thessalonians 5: 16-19 (KJV). Does that mean you should only ask and pray when you are in trouble or facing many challenges? No. The Word of God tells us that we should always stay in connection with Jesus Christ, for He is our provider and knows about all of our needs. Paul was encouraging the believers in Thessalonica, when he felt their faith was low. No matter the situation they were facing, he encouraged them to seek God first and pray without ceasing, because God alone knew what they needed. Therefore, he asked them to turn all of their attention to God and not away from Him.

While facing my challenges, it was easy for me to become resistant to listening to the voice of God. However, once I changed my prayer life, I saw the plans God had for me in a new way. God was always there taking care of my needs. I had to change my prayer life and seek after Him regularly. I want to encourage you to stop turning away for whatever the reason may be. Learn to place yourself in position to listen to His voice and let Him pour into you. This is achieved through prayer and constantly seeking after God. He will show up for you. Be consistent in your prayer life, seek Him daily, and you will see more of the plans God has for you. Be encouraged. Amen.

EMPOWERING YOUR FAITH

As your prayer life changes, your faith will become empowered. Empowering your faith will help to increase your strength, and keep you from resisting the voice of God. When I was facing my challenges, had no hope, felt weak and lost to my surroundings, and was unable to see my situation changing in front of me, I recognized that my faith was not strong. I needed a serious reboot. I was reminded of that with a very familiar verse in the Gospel according to Matthew, where he says, "We should have faith the size of a mustard seed." I remember saying to myself after reading this verse, "I have faith as small as a mustard seed, but only to feel later after deep reflection that, there was no root, no belief to this level of faith." So what was holding me back?

I turned again to the Gospel of Matthew, where he says, "Jesus answered and said unto them, verily I say unto you, if ye have faith, and doubt not, ye shall not only do this which is done to the fig tree, but also if ye shall say unto this mountain, Be thou removed, and be thou cast into the sea; it shall be done. And all things whatsoever ye shall ask in prayer, believing, ye shall receive." Matthew 21: 21-22 (KJV) This portion of scriptures teaches us that we have the authority to speak to our situation, but have to take the word to heart. There is no room for doubt. We have the power given to us by God, the One, who is faithful to His promises – the One who takes care of us. We can conquer the things that try to conquer us. And what we must understand is that our faith has to be empowered so that we can use the authority granted to us by God to overcome our challenges and to stand firm and strong no matter what comes our way.

Building up your faith helps to empower you and makes you stronger in dealing with the pressures of life. I encourage you to take some time out of your life and daily routine to be in the presence of God and deal with the challenges of life with God in prayer. It is in those times where you learn to trust God to be part of your everyday life. When you come to know more about God. But it takes "mustard seed faith" to get there. Now, as you seek God, ask Him to help you develop a strong prayer life, study His word, and meditate on the things He reveals to you. When you do, I guarantee you that your life's challenges will no longer consume you and cause you to resist listening to the voice of God anymore. Be encouraged.

Meditation

There are quite a few spiritual disciplines that can help you practice listening to the voice of God. Meditation is an integral part of your journey in listening to the voice of God. How does meditation help you *not* be resistant to listening to His voice? It will train you to focus and know the difference in distinguishing the voice of God. It is a powerful tool within the spiritual disciplines, and not only helps you focus on God, but helps to better your life. As you seek God in developing your prayer life, include meditation as part of your daily prayer journey.

Reflection

The resistance I experienced when not listening to the voice of God made me feel as if I was in a tug-of-war with God. Have you ever felt like you are in a tug-of- war with God when it comes to listening to His voice?

_____

_____

_____

_____

When it comes to resistance to the voice of God, have you asked yourself what steps you need to take to stop resisting Him?

_____

_____

_____

_____

Discovering God

During our time of resisting His voice, it can be difficult to surrender to Him, because we have so many things distracting us: our jobs, our families, our business. But what I have come to understand is that when I choose not to make time for God, I suffer more from the things that are weighing down on me. God still has the ability to speak to us, but what better way to receive than to be opened to hearing it? Our resistance to hearing and our constantly putting things in the way, which even includes our problems, can cause us to miss the blessings God has in store for us. I encourage you to work through the things that cause you to resist God and ask Him to help you listen to His word so that you will be open to receiving the blessings that have been named for you.

Scripture

Matthew 4:4—"But He answered and said, It is written, Man shall not live by bread alone, but by every word that proceedeth out of the mouth of God." (KJV)

Joshua 1:8—"This book of the law shall not depart out of thy mouth; but thou shalt meditate therein day and night, that thou mayest observe to do according to all that is written there- in: for then thou shalt make thy way prosperous, and then thou shalt have good success." (KJV)

Romans 8:15—"For ye have not received the spirit of bondage again to fear; but ye have received the Spirit of adoption, whereby we cry, Abba, Father." (KJV)

Prayer

Lord Jesus, I am grateful to be in Your presence one more time. I seek to be more like You, and to listen to Your voice teaching me to "meditate therein day and night." Jesus, in my meditation, I have learned to trust You more and more. During my quiet time with You, Lord, I want to experience You more. In my quiet time, Lord, I will hear Your voice. Help me, Lord, when I hear Your voice, not to be afraid, but to run toward You even more. As I continue to seek You more, I am open to listening to Your voice. I do not want to resist Your will. Lord, I pray this prayer in Your name. Let the words of my mouth and the meditation of my heart be glorified in You. In Jesus' name, I pray. Amen, amen, and amen.

Chapter Three

NEGLECTING TO OBEY WHAT GOD SAYS IS DANGEROUS

Whoso despiseth the word shall be destroyed: but he that feareth the commandment shall be rewarded.

– Proverbs 13:13

When God is calling, we cannot just simply ignore Him.

There is danger in choosing *not* to yield to God's voice. Instead, accept what He is trying to tell you, listen to His correction and reproof, submit to His commissioning of you, open yourself up to Him, and allow Him to pour into you. The Bible has plenty of examples of those who refused to listen to God and rejected what He had spoken. Just look at Jonah, who went in the opposite direction of where God instructed him to go. Let's not forget about Abraham, who was told by God that he would have the promise of a child, but took matters into his own hands and did not believe what God had spoken. Whatever the case may be, God expects us to listen to and follow the what He speaks to us. Refusing to do so causes a lot of problems and consequences.

When we neglect what God says to us, we go against His will. God's will for us to experience and eternal reward is His ultimate plan for us. However, when we go against Him, we are in danger of not receiving His rewards. The enemy makes it seem impossible to follow God's will when we face challenges such as the loss of a job, financial difficulties, relationship issues and other hard times. No matter the challenges that we are faced with, we want to be in a place to listen to God and be accepting of His plans for each of us, regardless of how difficult it may seem at times. Neglecting what God is saying can be dangerous because we will not be the recipients and inheritors of His promises. It also puts our souls in jeopardy, has us living in constant fear and terror of what might happen to us because we did not obey, and takes away the possibility of experiencing the joyous reward of eternal life. The word of God says,

> Because I have called, and ye refused, I have stretched out my hand, and no man regarded, But ye have set at nought all my counsel, and would none of my reproof. I also will laugh at your calamity I will mock when your fear cometh; when you fear cometh as desolation, and your destruction cometh as a whirlwind; when distress and anguish cometh upon you. Then shall they call upon me, but I will not answer, they shall seek me early, but they shall not find me. For that they hated knowledge, and did not choose the fear of the Lord. They would none of my counsel: they despised

all my reproof. Therefore shall they eat of the fruit of their own way, and be filled with their own devices. For the turning away of the simple shall slay them, and the prosperity of fools shall destroy them. But whoso hearkeneth unto me shall dwell safely, and shall be quiet from fear of evil. Proverbs 1:24–33 (KJV]

This is a heavy truth to bear, You may say to yourself, "Why does it have to get to this point?" The uncertainty captured in the Book of Proverbs is designed to help us see why we should be in partnership with God and abide by the things He is calling us to do. Doing so requires us to be open to listening to Him. And still, it is one thing to listen, but it is another thing to follow what has been spoken. You can see what happens when we do not listen. I encourage you to develop a true partnership with God.

What you have to remember is that His calling of you has a purpose. The calling can be to bring you out of a situation, to deliver you from some element that is disturbing your life, to be a means of inspiration in the life of someone that has been broken deeper than you, to be a shining light in a dark place, to be an answer to someone's problem, to be a symbol of hope in an area that is perishing, to deliver a message of promise, or just to get the healing that requires you to surrender to God. Our disobedience can be a penalize us and others. When you neglect to obey the voice of God, danger comes in.

Meditation

When God finally speaks to you and you choose not
to listen, you place yourself in danger of forfeiting the promises that
God has waiting for you, and of destroying the good plans that He
has for you to be a blessing to the people to whom He is calling you.
To avoid this, it is much better to receive than to resist. God has what
is best for you, but you have to allow Him in, and accept what He is
calling you to do. Rest at God's feet. Meditate and get connected to
God so He can reveal what is making you uncertain and afraid.
Meditation helps you focus. When you meditate, God talks to you
inside your mind and helps you work through the barriers that keep
you running in the other direction – away from God. Look at Jonah,
for instance. He was called by God to warn the people of Ninevah of
the coming destruction but did not want to do the command of God,
to go to the city of Ninevah. He decided not to accept what God was
saying. Neglecting to accept God's voice, he followed his own will,
and because he traveled in the opposite direction, he found himself
in more danger. Jonah neglected to accept what God was saying, was
swallowed by a fish, and spent three days

and three nights in the belly of the fish. He refused to allow God's plan to work through him, but instead opposed the plans God had spoken to him and turned in another direction. As a result, he experienced God's chastisement and was disciplined because of his actions. He also endangered others when he neglected to accept what God had said. Jonah learned the hard way, what happens when we do not accept God's directions. Eventually, he surrendered to what God said and was obedient to what God wanted of him. While our actions may not be the same as Jonah's, not listening to what God says will cause a battle. You will not win. You will miss out on the blessings God has for you and others—blessings which can only come when you yield to the ministry God is calling you to.

The Bible encourages meditation. Set aside times to meditate or reflect to help you accept what God is saying. Psalm 46:10 says, *"Be still, and know that I am God: I will be exalted among the heathen, I will be exalted in the earth."* (KJV) Be reminded that God wants you to develop a partnership with Him and accept what He is saying to you. He does not want you to experience the consequences of knowing, but not heeding His voice.

Reflection

When I choose not to accept God, who suffers from my choice?

_____

_____

_____

_____

You may be wrestling with what God is saying. In what ways can you manage those feelings to ensure that you do not neglect what God is saying and to ensure that you avoid the consequences of choosing to disregard His prompting?

_____

_____

_____

_____

Discovering God

Wrestling with accepting what God is saying to you can place you in an awkward and uncomfortable position, but if you get in a habit of waiting to hear His voice, He can share with you why He is calling you. It is through developing a relationship with God that we get an understanding of why He calls us and what we must do. If we can learn to trust in His leading and move beyond the doubting and resisting, we can see the beauty and the need for the calling.

Put yourself in a position to be in relationship with God, and do not neglect it, because it can be the very thing that is needed for your life. Nonetheless, you will never know if you choose to turn away. Work toward learning to be obedient and yielding to His voice, and allow God to reveal what He needs you to hear. Take some time out of your schedule to meditate with Him and accept what He is saying, because the outcomes can be gratifying. I sincerely hope you will not miss the opportunity to be a blessing to others and a recipient of the blessings that God has for you.

Scripture

Proverbs 3:5-6—"Trust in the Lord with all thine heart; and lean not unto thine own understanding. In all thy ways acknowledge Him, and He shall direct thy paths." (KJV)

Job 33:14—"For God speaketh once, yea twice, yet man perceiveth it not." (KJV)

Hebrews 2:3—"How shall we escape, if we neglect so great salvation; which at the first began to be spoken by the Lord, and was confirmed unto us by them that heard Him." (KJV)

Prayer

Father, You are good, and Your steadfast love endures forever.

I worship You always. I thank you for giving me the victory and abundant life in Jesus Christ, although I don't deserve it. You pour out to me with unconditional love and forgiveness. Father, as I learn to accept what You are saying, I want to thank you for comforting me and blessing me in the presence of my enemies. For this, Lord, I will shout for joy. Lord, I want to be in the right place not to experience the dangers in neglecting Your will. Lord, being in Your presence allows me to understand that nothing compares to You and that no weapon can stand against You. My desire is to follow You, because in all things, I am more than a conqueror through You. Heavenly Father, I pray this prayer in Your Son's name. Let the words of my mouth and the meditations of my heart be acceptable to You. Amen, amen, and amen.

Chapter Four

LEARN TO SURRENDER TO WHAT YOU HEARD GOD SPEAK

So then faith cometh by hearing, and hearing by
the word of God.
– Romans 10:17

The Merriam-Webster dictionary defines the word

surrender as, "to yield to the power, control, or giving up the possession of something, especially into the power of another." Spiritual surrender means that as a believer, you have entirely given up your will to the will of God. Paul's letter to the Philippi in Philippians 1:21 expresses that, "For to me to live is Christ, and to die is gain." Paul was not speaking of natural death; instead, he was speaking of spiritual death. Once you have accepted and surrendered to Christ, you are in the position to hear God speak.

When we surrender to God, we open ourselves to His will and surrender our will for how life should be lived in order to find true life in Him. In partnership with God, and through this intimate fellowship, we come to know who we truly are from God's perspective. But it requires an act of surrender. The Scripture says, "For I know the thoughts that I think toward you, saith the Lord, thoughts of peace, and not of evil, to give you an expected end" Jeremiah 29:11 (KJV). The Word of God clearly states that God knows the plans He has for us; therefore, we should not be afraid to surrender to hear what He is saying to us. And it is true to say that this will not always be easy, because the enemy will try to crowd our minds with fear. The enemy wants to make it difficult for us to hear what God is saying. Why? Because the enemy is threatened by the possibilities of our lives shifting from the traps, lies, and deception he has made us believe. His plans are to steal and rob us of the joy, peace, and love our heavenly Father created for us. We are reminded of this in John 10:10: "The thief cometh not, but for to steal, and to kill, and to destroy: I am come that they might have life, and that they might have it more abundantly." We have to guard ourselves with the scriptures as our weapon against the enemy's snares, by using the Word of God to counteract anything the enemy tries to distract us with. His will allows us to be victorious over the enemy's mind games and schemes.

In my most challenging moments, I have learned to surrender all to God. It is absolutely vital for me to hear what He is saying to me. Surrendering to God is good, because in Him, there is true life. When you surrender to God, you are letting the enemy know that you no longer belong to him and that the lies he has told you all your life have no hold on you. I'd gone through a period of depression, hardships, and difficulties, nonetheless, when I finally opened myself up to God, I was able to get to the place where I could hear Him speaking so softly and tenderly to me. God comforted me when I yielded. I knew then that I was ready to surrender my all to Him. In learning to hear and surrender to what God was saying to me, I had to practice centering myself in His presence. I'd center myself by sitting quietly at His feet and being open to God pouring into me. The more I spent time with God, at His feet and resting in His presence, the less distracted I was. God disciplined me. Because of my experience, I encourage you to find the time and a quiet place to be in His presence. If you have never practiced centering prayer, I would like to share some meditation scriptures that I use in my centering time with God.

- Exodus 33:15—"And he said unto Him, if thy presence go not with me, carry us not up hence." According to Moses, his centering prayer would be this: "Lord, if you don't go with us or before us, we are not going anywhere."
- Genesis 22:8—"And Abraham said, My son, God will provide himself a lamb for a burnt offering: so they went both of them together." Abraham's centering prayer would be, "The Lord will provide."

- Genesis 32:26—"And he said, Let me go, for the day breaketh. And he said, I will not let thee go, except thou bless me." Jacob's centering prayer was, "I won't let go of you unless you bless me."

- Joshua 24:15—"And if it seem evil unto you to serve the Lord, choose you this day whom ye will serve; whether the gods which your fathers served that were on the other side of the flood, or the gods of the Amorites, in whose land ye dwell: but as for me and my house, we will serve the Lord." Joshua would say, "As for me and my house, we will serve the Lord."

- 1 Samuel 3:10—"And the Lord came, and stood, and called as at other times, Samuel, Samuel. Then Samuel answered, Speak; for thy servant heareth." Samuel's centering prayer was, "Speak, Lord, for your servant is listening."

- Nehemiah 8:10—"Then he said unto them, God your way, eat the fate, and drink the sweet, and send portions unto them for whom nothing is prepared: for this day is Holy unto our Lord: neither by ye sorry; for the joy of the Lord is your strength." Nehemiah would say, "The joy of the Lord is my strength."

- Psalm 23:1—"The Lord is my shepherd; I shall not want." David, in his centering prayer, would say, "The Lord is my Shepherd, I shall not want," and in Psalm "This is the day which the Lord hath made; we will rejoice and be glad in it." David would continue in his centering prayer with, "This is the day that the Lord has made and I will rejoice and be glad in it."

- 1 Chronicles 4:10—"And Jabez called on the God of Israel, saying, Oh that thou wouldest bless me indeed, and enlarge my coast, and that thine hand might be with me, and that thou wouldest keep me from evil, that it may nor grieve me! And God grant- ed him that which he requested." Jabez' centering prayer would be, "Oh, that you may bless me and enlarge my territory."

I am not suggesting that scriptures are the only things you can use during your centering time. However, having scriptures, prayers, or worship with which to meditate when you begin your centering time practice is an essential way to help you to get to a place of surrendering yourself wholeheartedly in your quest to hear what God is saying to you. I believe the scriptures, God's Holy Word, has the power to do just that. The rewards come when you surrender all to Him and say, "Yes Lord, here I am." For His word reminds us to, "Trust in the Lord with all thine heart; and lean not unto thine own understanding. In all thy ways acknowledge Him, and He shall direct thy paths" Proverbs 3:5–6 (KJV). I encourage you, my brothers and sisters, trust God in the process of learning to hear, surrender, and obey everything you hear from Him.

Meditation

Today, as you practice your spiritual disciplines, settle your mind and soul and be open to what you hear God saying. Picture yourself as Mary sitting at Jesus' feet. Although Martha needed her help, Mary knew that her greater purpose, in that moment, was to be at Jesus' feet. Allow the Holy Spirit to take you to the place where you can hear the voice of God, sharing with you all that He desires. Let go and surrender everything to Him. If you find yourself crying, don't stop. Our tears are a language our Father knows. Let go and enter into His presence. Sit at His feet. Relax, for you are with your Father who knows you best.

Reflection

Has it been challenging for you to surrender to God's voice? Explain why you think it has been a challenge.

_____

_____

_____

_____

As you practice surrendering to God's voice, what is most challenging? List the challenges. Ask God to show you how to surrender even more and how to overcome the more challenging areas.

_____

_____

_____

_____

Discovering God

One of the hardest things for us to do in our spiritual journey is surrender all to God. No matter where God is calling you, whether it is to serve others, counsel others, or preach, it is never easy. Remember that you are hu- man. Despite how gifted or talented you are, you do not have control over everything. Part of hearing when God speaks is settling down take a moment away from all you are doing, being truthful with yourself in that moment, and realizing that you don't know everything. Relax, take a deep breath, and   say, "God, here I am. I thank You for gifting me with all these talents, but I cannot use them without your guidance." Don't forget, faith comes by hearing, and hearing comes by the word of God. Let go and surrender to what you hear God saying. Trust the process.

Scripture

Luke 10:39—"And she had a sister called Mary, which also sat at Jesus' feet, and heard his word." (KJV)

Galatians 2:20—"I am crucified with Christ: nevertheless live; yet not I, but Christ liveth in me: and the life which I now live in the flesh I live by the faith of the Son of God, who loved me, and gave himself for me." (KJV)

Psalms 9:10—"And they that know thy name will put their trust in thee: for thou, Lord, hast not forsaken them that seek thee." (KJV)

Prayer

Heavenly Father, I come to You, submitting all to You. Lord, I know the plan you have for me, and that is to give me great joy. Lord, help me get to the place where I understand how much I need You in everything I do. In the same way that Mary sat at your feet and felt such comfort, I want to experience joy and comfort with You. Teach me what it means to surrender all to You. My desire is to hear Your voice. So, Lord, I pray that as I wrestle with hearing Your voice that I will also trust you. Lord Jesus, I decree and declare for this breakthrough in your Name, Jesus, I pray. Let the words of my mouth and the meditation of my heart be with you always. Amen, amen, and amen.

Chapter Five

MOVE IN THE DIRECTION THAT GOD IS CALLING YOU

Shew me thy ways, O LORD; teach me thy paths.
- Psalm 25:4

The King James Version dictionary defines, the word "move" means to change place or pasture, to stir, to pass, or go in any manner or direction from one place or part of space to another. In Chapter 17 of The Book of Acts, the apostle expresses the word move to be an action. Acts 17:28 reads, "For in Him we live, and move, and have our being; as certain also of your own poets have said, For we are also his offspring." (KJV) We should be moving in the direction God is calling us to move. The first step in the process of moving in God's direction, according to the Apostle Paul, is to say, "Yes Lord, here I am." When God lives in us, He moves through us, but having God move in our lives requires us to surrender all to Him.

To move continuously in God's direction toward those places where He is calling you to requires:

- Consistent Prayer
  - Practice centering prayer. Doing this will help you to create a consistent prayer life.
- Daily Bible Study
  - Spend time studying the word of God every day.
- Practice the Sabbath.
  - Plan a day of rest from everything (phone, television, social media, etc.) and just be in the presence of God.

When you move in the direction that God is calling you to go, it can be a life-changing experience, but it can also be scary and uncomfortable. Please know that you are not alone. I encourage you to continue to trust God no matter what. In the Book of Proverbs, Solomon reminds us to, "Trust in the Lord with all thine heart; and lean not unto thine own understanding. In all thy ways acknowledge Him, and He shall direct thy paths." Proverbs 3:5-6 (KJV) As we set our hearts to move in the direction of God's voice, we must "trust God," with all of our hearts. Trusting in God in good times is different from trusting God when we are faced with life challenges. However, in all seasons of life, we should trust God with all of our hearts. That is why Solomon encourages us to be open with all of our heart to God, for in Him there is prosperity, health, and security. And God wants all of that for us.

There is a difference in our lives when we yield and surrender all to God. I was able to see the difference in myself. I stopped thinking that I could not accomplish my goals, and accepted that with God – I could. I trusted God even more with my life and moved in the direction He wanted me to go. I doubted in the beginning like so many others, such as Moses, Joshua, and Jeremiah. But what I have come to learn is that no matter my fears, God still had a plan, and although I was afraid, God was pressing me to get there. Like the Prophet Jeremiah says, "For I know the thoughts that I think toward you, saith the Lord, thoughts of peace, and not of evil, to give you an expected end." 29:11(KJV).

Knowing God's promises never fail made me confident enough to move in the direction God was calling me. Because I was convinced that God was in control, surrendering to Him was a rewarding process for me. I recognized that the enemy tries to plot and stop the plans of God when he tries to place fears and doubts in our minds. He tries to throw us off the path God is calling us to take. I experienced this, but learned to stand firm through it and to stay on course. I held fast to the scripture in Isaiah 54:17, which says, "No weapon that is formed against thee shall prosper; and every tongue that shall rise against thee in judgment thou shalt condemn. This is the heritage of the servants of the LORD, and their righteousness is of me, saith the LORD."

As you move in the direction God is calling you, I want to encourage you with the words of the psalmist, David, who said, "Search me, O God, and know my heart: try me, and know my thoughts: and see if there be any wicked way in me, and lead me in in the way everlasting." Psalm 139:23-24 (KJV) He asked God to search his heart because he knew God was in control. David surrendered to God searching his heart, because his love for God was true, deep, and passionate. While you are moving in the direction God is pointing you, try to imagine David asking God to search his heart. Imagine David surrendering all to God. Be open. Ask God to search your heart. Have the courage to go in the direction He predestined for you.

My prayer for you today, is that while you are surrendering and moving in God's direction that you will be open like the psalmist David. I pray that you will ask God to search your heart and that you will be open to the process. Obey, have faith and a beautiful change burst forth in your life.

Meditation

In our meditation today, find a quiet place, turn off all phones and televisions, and sit where your feet touch the floor. The only thing you should have around you is your Bible, your notebook, and your journal. Now, let us position ourselves to be in His presence. If you like have soothing music playing in the background, make sure it's not too loud. If it is too silent for you, have waterfall musical playing very slow. Remember, in the stillness, you want to hear God's directions and move toward Him. Our Father enjoys spending time with us and looks forward to us sharing time with Him. Ask Him to show you the way and teach you His path as you move in His direction for you.

Reflection

To Move in the direction that God is calling you, we have to learn to trust Him with every area of our life. Ask yourself, Am I ready to trust God with every area of my life?

_____

_____

_____

_____

God desires to have a close relationship with us. Are you ready to say, "Yes, Lord, here I am"? Specifically what can you do to moving toward what He is calling you to do? Write them down.

_____

_____

_____

_____

Discovering God

Discovering God as we move in the direction He is calling us to move means trusting God's will for your life. When we are driving to a place we've never been before, we trust that our GPS is going to take us from point A to point B. In the same way, trust that God, who knows the plans He's mapped out for you, will get you from point A to point B. Understand that without God leading and directing you, you are going to be lost.

When we have no clue where we are going; we put our trust in the GPS for directions. Why not surrender to the One who knows and provides everything for you? Why not move in the direction He is calling you? Go, now.

Scripture

Psalm 32:8-9—"I will instruct thee and teach thee in the way which thou shalt go: I will guide thee with mine eye. Be ye not as the horse, or as the mule, which have no understanding: whose mouth must be held in with bit and bridle, lest they come near unto thee." (KJV)

Psalm 16:7-8—"I will bless the LORD, who hath given me counsel: my reins also instruct me in the night seasons. I have set the LORD always before me: because he is at my right hand, I shall not be moved." (KJV)

John 16:13—"Howbeit when he, the Spirit of truth, is come, he will guide you into all truth: for he shall not speak of himself; but whatsoever he shall hear, that shall he speak: and he will shew you things to come." (KJV)

Prayer

Eternal Father, I thank You for seeing me as worthy to be called one of Your servants. Lord, I am grateful for Your guidance as I move toward the ministry You have called me to. I may not see myself as worthy, but Your word says, "Shew me thy ways," and Your ways are what I want to know and come into fellowship with. So, Lord, in my surrendering all to You, I am asking You, Lord Jesus, to teach me the right way. Lord, the paths can be lonely, but I have come to place my trust in You, and I know, Lord Jesus, that I am going to be okay. As I obey You, I am assured of Your love toward me. Without any shadow of a doubt, I accept and move in the direction where You are calling me. I submit to Your Will and not to my own. I pray this prayer and seal it with Your blood, in Jesus' Name. Let the words of my mouth and the meditation of my heart be acceptable in thy sight, I pray. Amen, amen, and amen.

Chapter Six

OBEY THE VOICE OF GOD

I delight to do thy will, O my God: yea,

thy law is within my heart.

– Psalm 40:8

The King James Version dictionary defines the word

obedient as "submissive to authority, yielding compliance with commands, orders or injunctions, performing what is required, or abstaining from what is forbidden."

The Bible, from Genesis to Revelation, speaks of obedience. Deuteronomy 11:26-28 says, "Behold, I set before you this day a blessing and a curse; a blessing, if ye obey the commandments of the Lord your God, which I command you this day: And a curse, if ye will not obey the commandments of the Lord your God, but turn aside out of the way which I command you this day, to go after other gods, which ye have not known." John 14:15 says, "If you love me, keep my commandments.". Both Scriptures help us to understand the result of being obedient to the voice of God.

Both the King James Version dictionary and scriptures help us to understand the outcome when you are not obedient to the voice of God. To be obedient to God's voice, one should be humble and patient, and spend time in His presence. Many of us, if we are honest, struggle with one or all three of these areas. Can I be truthful with you? I have struggled with all three areas. I am a multitasking person and like seeing things done in the right way. I struggled big time being patient, to the point that I would instead complete the project on my own and not wait on someone else to get the job done. I also lived a busy life. I always had a busy schedule, with so much to do and that made it difficult for me to be faithfully committed to God. I was not taking the time to spend in God's presence. It was not until I had what I call my 360 degree experience. This was when I realized the importance of spending time in His presence. I saw the big picture once I yielded and surrendered my all to God. It was then that I witnessed the results of being obedient to the voice of God. I encourage you to, as Moses did with the Israelite people, obey God. You will be blessed.

However, if you disobey God, you will be cursed and lose out on the wonderful gifts and plans He has for you. Once you learn that God's will for your life is the best, your true meaning and purpose will be revealed. Rest assured that this revelation requires that you align yourself according to His plans for you. We can easily miss His plan and purpose for our lives when we chose not to be obedient to the voice of God. My brothers and sisters, I want to encourage you to spend time in God's presence. As you are practicing this time of surrendering to God and being obedient to Him, you will learn to hear His voice. Be humble and patient; God is humble and patient with us. Being in the company and fellowship of God is rewarding and amazing. Prepare, as you obey, to see the plans of God overflow before your eyes.

I encourage you to surrender all to God today. Say, "Yes, Lord. Here I am," and you will receive the everlasting life that the Gospel of John tells us is the result of being obedient.

Meditation

Contemplative prayer helps us as we focus on a word and repeat that word over and over in meditation practice. It helps to clear your mind of outside concerns so that the voice of God can more easily be heard. As we obey the voice of God, this practice helps us to say yes. Saying yes is part of how we practice obedience to the voice of God. As you continue in your spiritual disciplines, remain open to the voice of God and surrender all to Him.

Reflection

What is preventing you from saying yes right now?

_____

_____

_____

_____

Saying yes to the voice of God requires us to be obedient. Psalm 40:8 says, "I delight to do thy will, O my God: yea, they law is within my heart." How far are you right now, from being able to obey the will of God?

_____

_____

_____

_____

Discovering God

God is always speaking to us, because He wants us to have that intimate relationship with Him. That is the way it should be. He created us in His own image. Once you accept Christ as your Lord and Savior, the Holy Spirit becomes alive in you. Nothing should prevent us from saying yes to the voice of God. It is through Him that we are free. God does not look at our faults and push us away. In our faults, God reaches out to us even more. His love for us never changes. Take a look at His Son. He sent His only Son to die for us so that we can be free. Now, remind me once again why you cannot say yes and be obedient to the voice of God?

Scripture

Deuteronomy 5:33—"Ye shall walk in all the ways which the LORD your God hath commanded you, that ye may live, and that it may be well with you, and that ye may prolong your days in the land which ye shall possess." (KJV)

1 Corinthians 15:58—"Therefore, my beloved brethren, be ye steadfast, unmoveable, always abounding in the work of the Lord, forasmuch as ye know that your labour is not in vain in the Lord." (KJV)

Joshua 1:18—"Whosoever he be that doth rebel against thy commandment, and will not hearken unto thy words in all that thou commandest him, he shall be put to death: only be strong and of a good courage." (KJV)

Prayer

Heavenly Father, I thank You for all of Your promises to us. Eternal Father, You said that if we walked in obedience, we would receive abundance, grace, and a full life with You, Lord Jesus. Once we are obedient, we will receive an overflow of blessings in our lives, for our children, and for generations and generations to come.

Your word says in Deuteronomy that if we obey, we will be blessed, but if we disobey, we will be cursed. Lord Jesus, help us not to be disobedient or rebel against You. Your word clearly states that when we disobey, we are rejecting everlasting life with You in the Heavenly Kingdom.

Lord Jesus, please help us to have a humble spirit and to yield and surrender to Your will.

Lord Jesus, thank You for these blessings. I decree and declare in our surrendering all, that our answer will be "Yes, Lord, Here I am." I am open to accepting Your will and the directions You have for me. Let the words of my mouth and the meditation of my heart be acceptable in thy sight. In Jesus' name, I pray. Amen, amen, and amen.

Chapter Seven

ENCOURAGE OTHERS TO OBEY THE VOICE OF GOD

I will run the way of thy commandments, when
thou shalt enlarge my heart.
- Psalm 119:32

Finally, in my process of answering, "Yes Lord, here I am," I was able to run toward God's prompting. Now, I am here to encourage you not to be afraid to surrender all to God. As part of your process of surrendering your all to God, you must learn to, "Trust God and trust the process." In the Book of James, he shares that, *"If any of you lack wisdom, let him ask of God, that giveth to all men liberally, and upbraideth not, and it shall be given him."* James 1:5.

James encourages us to understand the purpose of why we should run toward God's prompting. Exercising *wisdom* is required for us surrendering to God as He reveals his plans and purpose for our lives. This is why, as James reminds us, "We should ask because God is the giver." No matter what has happened in your past, God, who is the giver and fulfiller of promises, will take care of you. God is concerned about the things you need and He wants the best for you. He also wants to be the hand that guides you along in the process of experiencing the fullness of what was envisioned for you from the beginning.

God will not allow anything to stand in your way. Therefore, you should not allow anything to stand in your way. Trust in God and your life will be opened to His outpouring. Trust in God as He moves you in the direction He is prompting you, for we all have a calling in our lives. Though it may not be the same as another, we have been called and the reward is the same for us all. It is the reward of eternal life when we surrender, are obedient, and move in the direction God is steering you.

I encourage you to accept the change and be transparent by surrendering everything to God. I am living and walking in the plans He has for me because I learned to "Trust God and Trust the Process." Timothy shares, "Who hath saved us, and called us with a holy calling, not according to our works, but according to His own purpose and grace, which was given us in Christ Jesus before the world began" 2 Timothy 1:9. Developing an intimate relationship with Him comes when we trust God as we run toward Him. I have so much to be thankful to God for. If you, too, are grateful for all God has done, I encourage you to let nothing stop you from running toward Him. Like the Prophet Jeremiah, God knows the plans He has for us. *"Before I formed thee in the belly I knew thee; and before thou camest forth out of the womb I sanctified thee, and I ordained thee a prophet unto the nations."* Jeremiah 1:5 (KJV). I encourage you to run toward the direction that God is calling you, and trust His plans. I challenge you today to ask yourself this question: How can I reap all the rewards God has for me? Then allow your inner self to be open when you say, "Yes, Lord, Here I am. And I surrender all to you, God."

God plans and love for us is so holy, pure, and true. This is evident, because He sent His Son, Christ Jesus, to die for our sins so that we could have everlasting life with Him. I encourage you not to be discouraged by the things of this world, no matter how challenging they may seem, but be open to God's voice and release it all to Him.

The prophet Jeremiah wrestled with running toward God's prompting; likewise, it is okay for us to wrestle as we run toward God's prompting. God knew you before you were formed in your mother's womb. I encourage you, amid your wrestling, to be willing to open yourself to God and run toward His prompting. "Trust God and Trust the Process." God does not call the equipped; He equips the ones He calls. I encourage you, while you are preparing yourself to answer and even when while you wrestle with the calling—respond. When you put your trust in His hands, you will experience the reward of life as God ordained it to be for you.

Meditation

The use of spiritual disciplines will teach you to be in the presence of God and to hear His voice. Contemplative prayer is having a close spiritual union with God. Sit with God, stay in His presence, and wrestle with your calling as you seek Him daily. Paul says in 1 Corinthians 14:15, "What is it then? I will pray with the spirit, and I will pray with the understanding also: I will sing with the spirit, and I will sing with the understanding also." (KJV) God wants us to spend time with Him, and contemplative prayer will help you to do that. "Be careful for nothing; but in everything by prayer and supplication with thanksgiving let your requests be made known unto God." Philippians 4:6 (KJV) My brothers and sisters, let us trust God with our whole heart, so we can reap our full rewards.

Reflection

Think back to a time you knew God was prompting you to do something you may have thought was impossible. How did you feel? Were you open to His voice?

_____

_____

_____

_____

Are you ready to be open to your calling? Be honest, and list three areas preventing you from running to God's prompting. Surrender them to God and ask Him for His guidance.

_____

_____

_____

_____

Discovering God

In seeking God, we want to release everything. Lay it out all on the table. Know that God knows our hearts and our desires, and trust in His promises and favor toward us. Be open to God. Have a conversation with Him. Wrestle with your calling, let go of the fears and the doubts. Trust God with every part of your body. Remember Moses, who wrestled with the same questions. God reminded Moses and comforted him at the same time. "And Moses said unto the Lord, O my Lord, I am not eloquent, neither heretofore, nor since thou hast spoken unto thy servant: but I am slow of speech, and of a slow tongue. And the Lord said unto him, Who hath made man's mouth? Or who market the dumb, or dead, or the seeing, or the blind? Have not I the Lord? Now therefore go, and I will be with thy mouth, and teach thee what thou shalt say." Exodus 4:10-12 (KJV) Moses had to learn to trust God as he answered to God's calling, saying, "Yes Lord, Here I am." Now go and discover what God is prompting *you* to do. Surrender all to Him.

Scripture

Psalm 31:1—"In thee, O LORD, do I put my trust; let me never be ashamed: deliver me in thy righteousness." (KJV)

Psalm 141:8—"But mine eyes are unto thee, O GOD the Lord: in thee is my trust; leave not my soul destitute." (KJV)

Psalm 37:4-6—"Delight thyself also in the LORD; and He shall give thee the desires of thine heart. Commit thy way unto the LORD; trust also in Him; and He shall bring it to pass. And He shall bring forth thy righteousness as the light, and thy judgment as the noonday." (KJV)

Prayer

Eternal Father, I thank You for Your grace and mercy toward us. Your word says, if we delight in you Lord, You will give us the desires of our hearts. Right now, Lord, I seek You wholeheartedly, running to you, surrendering all to you. Today, Lord, I am saying, "Yes Lord. Here I am." I surrender to your calling. Heavenly Father, I run to You, seeking Your guidance as I hear Your voice. Lord Jesus, I pray this prayer and I pray that I will be bound and sealed with your blood. I can easily say thank You and I am grateful for Your love and care toward me. Let the words of my mouth and the meditation of my heart find You, in Jesus' name I pray. Amen, amen, and amen.

Conclusion

WE REACH THE END OF OUR JOURNEY, ONLY TO BEGIN THE TRUE ONE

Prayer of Encouragement

Have not I commanded thee? Be strong and of a good courage; be not afraid, neither be thou dismayed: for the Lord thy God is with thee whithersoever thou goest.

– Joshua 1:9

As you are surrendering to the voice of God, I encourage you to develop a daily prayer life. Believe in our God, who is the sole provider of all of your needs. He will guide you along the path because He is Jehovah.

- Jehovah—Jireh: The Lord who provides and my vision Genesis 2

- Jehovah—Rapha: The Lord who heals
  Exodus 15:22-26
- Jehovah—Nissi: The Lord our Banner Exodus 17:8-1
- Jehovah—El-Shaddai: He supply Genesis 17:3
- Jehovah—Shalom: The Lord is peace Judges 6:24
- Jehovah—Shammah: The Lord is there Ezekiel 48:35

Lord Jesus, I thank You for everyone who will come to hear Your voice as they are surrendering to You. I pray that every- one's prayer life will be different as they seek to have a deeper and more intimate relationship with You. I pray Your will be done as they come to the place of hearing and as they run to- ward Your voice. Lord Jesus, I pray for anyone who may feel that they don't know how to pray. May they believe as they pray the prayer, Jesus told His disciples to pray.

Our Father which art in Heaven, hallowed be thy Name. Thy Kingdom come. Thy will be done in earth, as it is in Heaven. Give us this day our daily bread. And forgive us our debts, as we forgive our debtors. And lead us not into temptation, but deliver us from evil: For thine is the Kingdom, and the power, and the glory, forever. Amen.

Lord Jesus, thank You for knowing our needs before we ask, and for supplying and providing for our needs. I pray, Lord, as they run toward Your voice, crying, "Abba, Father, I surrendered all to You," that in the midst of them crying, their answer will be, "Yes Lord, here I am." Lord Jesus, I pray for a hedge of protection to surround them as they move toward the prompting of Your voice. I pray for everyone to be open to the plans You have for them. I bind any known and unknown spirit that will interfere with Your will. I decree and declare, that doubt and fear will no longer be a hindrance to them as they run toward Your voice. I pray, our Lord and Savior Christ Jesus, enable them to fully surrender to Your divine calling.

Lord, I thank You for the change in everyone's life. Lord, I thank You for Your inspiration in writing this book to encourage others to run toward Your voice. I thank you Lord Jesus for the many lives that will answer and run toward the prompting of Your voice. Lord Jesus, I thank you for caring about us and all of our needs. I thank You, Lord, as we wrestle through our calling, for You cover and protect us daily. I thank You, Lord Jesus, for equipping us for the journey. I am grateful. I thank You, Lord Jesus, for our wrestling seasons, because it is during these times we learn to trust and surrender all to You. I declare Your will, in the mighty name of Jesus. Amen, amen, and amen.

Take your place now.
RUN. GOD IS WAITING FOR YOU!

About the Author

In 2013, when Joan accepted her

calling as an Evangelist, little did she know
the magnitude of the plans that God had
for her life. Joan grew up in the church but
would often say, *"I was brought up in the
church all my life, but after a while, the Church
was not in me."*

Nonetheless, just like God told the
prophet, Jeremiah, "Before I formed thee in the belly I knew thee,
and before thou camest forth out of the womb I sanctified thee."
God gave Joan just enough time to explore her options and to run
from her call, and in His perfect time, she yielded and surrendered to
Him.

Joan owes all her changes to the One and Only, the Almighty God,
who is head of her life. He is head of her life and her family, and she is
open to what God has for her. She believes God has prepared and
equipped her to go out and preached His Gospel to lost souls.

Joan loves God and loves studying His word. Joan says that studying God's word brings such a refreshing and rewarding feeling that draws her closer to Him each day. Her favorite Scripture is Isaiah 41:10: "Fear thou not; for I am with thee: be not dismayed; for I am thy God: I will strengthen thee; yea, I will help thee; yea, I will uphold thee with the right hand of my righteousness."

Joan stands still within God, and is grateful that He continues to take her through the process. The songs that help her to focus on where God is taking her are: **"I Won't Go Back"** by William McDowell and **"I'll Just Say Yes"** by Brian Courtney Wilson.

She is open and willing to surrender to wherever God calls her. As Joan often says, "Trust God and Trust the Process."